Hittel on Gold Mines and Mining

By

John S. Hittell

Hittel on Gold Mines and Mining
by John S. Hittell

ISBN: 978-93-62204-47-9

Published by

DOUBLE 9 BOOKS

2/13-B, Ansari Road
Daryaganj, New Delhi – 110002
info@double9books.com
www.double9books.com
Tel. 011-40042856

ABOUT THE AUTHOR

John S. Hittell was a distinguished American author and historian known for his comprehensive works on the history and culture of California. His masterpiece, "Hittel on Gold Mines and Mining," stands as a seminal text in the field of mining literature. In this extensive tome, Hittell meticulously documents the California Gold Rush and its profound impact on the region's development and society. With meticulous research and vivid storytelling, he provides a detailed account of the discovery of gold, the influx of miners, and the economic, social, and environmental consequences of the gold rush. Hittell's work not only offers invaluable insights into the history of mining but also serves as a testament to the human spirit of exploration, perseverance, and ambition. Through his meticulous documentation and keen analysis, Hittell captures the essence of an era defined by dreams of wealth and opportunity, leaving a lasting legacy in the annals of American history and mining literature.

CONTENTS

HITTEL ON GOLD MINES AND MINING

Chief Industry.—Mining is the chief industry of California. It employs more men and pays larger average wages than any other branch of physical labor. Although it has been gradually decreasing in the amount of its production, in the profits to the individuals engaged in it, and in its relative importance in the business of the state, it is yet and will long continue to be the largest source of our wealth, and the basis to support the other kinds of occupation.

Metals obtained.—Our mines now wrought are of gold, silver, quicksilver, copper and coal. Ores of tin, lead, and antimony in large veins, beds of sulphur, alum and asphaltum; lakes of borax and springs of sulphate of magnesia, are also found in the state, but they are not wrought at the present time, though they will probably all become valuable in a few years. Platinum, iridium, and osmium are obtained with the gold in some of the placer mines, but are never found alone, nor are they ever the main object sought by the miner. The annual yield of our gold mines is about forty millions of dollars, of our quicksilver two millions of dollars. Our silver, copper and coal mines have been opened within a year, and their value is yet unknown. All our other mining is of little importance as compared with the gold.

Gold Mines.—Our gold mines are divided into placer and quartz. In the former, the metal is found imbedded in layers of earthy matter, such as clay, sand and gravel; in the latter it is incased in veins of rock. The methods of mining must be adapted to the size of the particles of gold, and the nature of the material in which they are found. In placer mining, the earthy matter containing the gold, called the "pay-dirt," is washed in water, which dissolves the clay and carries it off in solution, and the current sweeps away the sand, gravel and stones, while the gold, by reason of the higher specific gravity, remains in the channel or is caught with quicksilver. In quartz mining the auriferous rock is ground to a very fine powder, the gold in which is caught in quicksilver, or on the rough surface of a blanket, over which the fine material is borne by a stream of water. About two-thirds of our gold is obtained from the placers, and one-third from the quartz.

A mine is defined and generally understood to mean "a subterraneous work or excavation for obtaining metals, metallic ores or mineral substances;" but this definition does not apply to our placer mines, which are places where gold is taken from diluvial or alluvial deposits. Most of the work is not subterraneous; it is done in the full light of day. In some of the claims the pay-dirt lies within two feet of the surface; in others it lies much deeper, but all the superincumbent matter is swept away.

Water is the great agent of the placer miner; it is the element of his power; its amount is the measure of his work, and its cost is the measure of his profit. With an abundance of water he can wash every thing; without water he can do little or nothing. Placer mining is almost entirely mechanical, and of such a kind that no accuracy of workmanship or scientific or literary education is necessary to mastery in it. Amalgamation is a chemical process it is true, but it is so simple that after a few days' experience, the rudest laborer will manage it as well as the most thorough chemist.

It is impossible to ascertain the amount of gold which has been taken from the mines of California. Records have been kept of the sums manifested at the San Francisco Custom House, for exportation, and deposited for coinage in the mints of the United States; and there is also some knowledge of the amounts sent in bars and dust to England; but we have no account of the sums carried by passengers to foreign countries and coined elsewhere than at London, or used as jewelry, or of the amount now in circulation in this state. According to the books of the Custom House of San Francisco, the sums manifested for export were as follows:

In 1849, $4,921,250; in 1850, $27,676,346; in 1851, $42,582,695; in 1852, $46,586,134; in 1853, $57,331,034; in 1854, $51,328,653; in 1855, $45,182,631; in 1856, $48,887,543; in 1857, $48,976,697; in 1858, $47,548,025; in 1859, $47,640,462; in 1860, $42,303,345; in 1861, $40,639,089; a total of $551,603,904 in twelve years.

The exportation of gold commenced in 1848, but we have no record of the sums sent away in that year. Previous to 1854 very large sums were carried away by passengers, who gave no statement at the Custom House; since that year, the manifests show the exportation correctly within a few millions. I am entirely satisfied that the total gold yield of California has been not less than seven hundred millions of dollars; but I have not room here to state the reasons for this opinion. My estimate is considerably less than that of most business men of the state, and less than that made by Hunt's *Merchants' Magazine*. There was undoubtedly a regular increase in the annual yield of the mines from 1848 to the end of 1853; and there has been a gradual decrease since the beginning of 1854—a decrease perhaps not very regular but still certain. Since 1854 considerable sums exported from San Francisco, and included in our tables, came from mines beyond the limits of California, such as the mines in Southern Oregon, in the eastern part of Washington Territory, in British Columbia, and in Nevada Territory; and while the California gold yield has been decreasing, these extraneous supplies have been increasing. Several millions must be deducted from the annual shipments since 1858, for foreign gold. The gold yield will undoubtedly continue to fall, but to what point and at what rate no one can know. I believe that in 1870, the yield will not exceed thirty millions of dollars.

Placer Mines. — Placer mines are divided into many classifications. The first and most important is into deep and shallow. In the former the pay-dirt is found deep, twenty feet or more beneath the surface; in the latter, near the surface. The shallow or surface diggings are chiefly found in the beds of ravines and gullies, in the bars of rivers, and in shallow flats; the deep diggings are in hills and deep flats. The pay-dirt is usually covered by layers of barren dirt, which is sometimes washed, and sometimes left undisturbed, while the pay-dirt is taken out from beneath it through tunnels or shafts. So far as our present information goes, we have reason to believe that no gold country ever possessed so large an extent of paying placer mines, with the pay-dirt so near the surface, and with so many facilities for working them as California. In Australia the diggings are very deep and spotted, that is, the gold is unevenly distributed, and the supply of water for mining is scanty. In Siberia the winter is terribly cold during six months of the year. In Brazil the diggings were not so extensive nor so rich as in this state. Here we have numerous large streams coming down through the mining districts, very large bodies of pay-dirt, and a mild climate.

After dividing placers into deep and shallow, the next classification will be according to their topographical position, as into hill, flat, bench, bar, river-bed, ancient river-bed, and gulch mines. Hill diggings are those where the pay-dirt is in or under a hill. Flat diggings are in a flat. Bench diggings are in a "bench" or narrow table on the side of a hill above a river. Benches of this kind are not uncommon in California, and they often indicate the place where the stream ran in some very remote age. Bars are low collections of sand and gravel at the side of a river and above its surface at low water. River-bed claims are those beneath the surface of the river at low water, and access is obtained to them only by removing the water from the bed by flumes or ditches. Ancient river-bed claims are those of which the gold was deposited by streams in places where no streams now exist. Gulch claims are those in gullies which have no water, save during a small part of the year. A "claim" is the mining land owned or held by one man or a company.

The placer mines are again classified according to the manner in which, or the instruments with which they are wrought. There are sluice claims, hydraulic claims, tunnel claims, dry washing, dry digging, and knife claims. In 1849 and 1850, the main classification of the placers was into wet diggings and dry diggings, the former meaning mines in the bars and beds of rivers, and dry diggings were those in gullies and flats where water could be obtained only part of the year or not at all. That classification was made while nearly all the mining was done near the surface, before the great deposits of pay-dirt in the hills had been discovered, and before ditches, sluices, and the hydraulic process had been introduced. The class of mines then known as the "dry diggings," and which for several years furnished nearly half of the gold yield of the state, are now, with a few unimportant exceptions, exhausted, or left to the attention of the Chinamen.

The purpose of all placer miners is not to catch all the gold in the dirt which they wash, but to catch the greatest possible quantity within a given time. It is not supposed that any process used in gold mining catches all the metal. Part of it is lost; in some processes a considerable proportion. The general estimate in California is, that one-twentieth of the gold in the dirt which is washed is lost. Many of the particles are so very small as to be invisible to the naked eye, and so light that their specific gravity does not avail to prevent them from being carried away by the water like sand. The larger pieces will sink to the bottom and resist the force of the water; the smaller the particles, the greater the danger that it will be borne away. Many devices have been tried to catch all the gold, but none have succeeded perfectly, and some which have caught a portion of what escaped from the ordinary modes of mining, have been found to cost more than their yield. The miner does not grieve about that which he cannot catch. He is not careful to catch all that he could. His purpose is to draw the largest possible revenue per day from his claim. He does not intend to spend many years in mining, or if he does, he has become thriftless and improvident. In either case, he wishes to derive the utmost immediate profit from his mine. If his claim contain a dollar to the ton, and he can save five dollars by slowly washing only six tons in a day, while he might make ten dollars by rapidly washing fifteen tons in a day, he will prefer the latter result, though he will loose twice as much of the precious metal by the fast as by the slow mode of working. The object of the miner is the practical dispatch of work, and his success will depend to a great extent upon the amount of dirt which he can wash within a given space of time. He regrets that any of the gold should be wasted, but his regret is because it escapes from his sluice and his pocket, rather than because it is lost to industry and commerce.

The Sluice. — The board-sluice is a long wooden trough, through which a constant stream of water runs, and into which the auriferous dirt is thrown. The water carries away the clay, sand, gravel and stones, and leaves the gold in the bottom of the sluice, where it is caught by its gravity and by quicksilver. The board-sluice is the great washing machine, and the most important instrument used in the placer mining of California. It washes nearly all the dirt and catches nearly all the placer gold of the country. It was invented here, although it had previously been used elsewhere; it has been more extensively employed here than in any other country, and it can be used here to more advantage than elsewhere. It is not less than fifty feet long, nor less than a foot wide, made of boards. The width is usually sixteen or eighteen inches; and never exceeds five feet. The length is ordinarily several hundred and sometimes several thousand feet. It is made in sections or "boxes" twelve or fourteen feet long. The boards are an inch and a half thick, and are sawn for that special purpose, the bottom boards being four inches wider at one end than the other. The narrow end of one box therefore fits in the wide end of another, and in that way the sluice is put together, a long succession of boxes, the lower end of each resting in the upper end of another, and not fastened together otherwise. These boxes stand upon trestles, with a descent varying from eight to eighteen inches in twelve feet. It is therefore an easy matter to put up or take down a sluice after the boxes are made, and it is not uncommon for the miners to haul their boxes from one claim to another. The descent of a sluice is usually the same throughout its length, and is called its "grade." If there be a fall of eight inches in twelve feet, the sluice has an "eight-inch grade," and if the fall be twice as great, it is a "sixteen-inch grade." The grade depends upon the character of the pay-dirt, the length of the sluice, and its position. The steeper the descent, the more rapidly the dirt is dissolved, but the greater the danger also that the fine particles of gold will be carried away by the water. The tougher the dirt, that is, the greater its resistance to the dissolving power of the water, the steeper, other things being equal, should be the sluice. A slow current does not dissolve tough clay, and that is the greater part of the pay-dirt, so rapidly as a swift one. The shorter the sluice, other things being equal, the smaller the grade should be. There is more danger that the fine particles of gold will be lost by a short sluice than by a longer one, and to diminish this danger, the rapidity of the current must be reduced by a small grade. The greater the amount of dirt to be washed, other things being equal, the steeper should be the grade; for a swift current will wash more dirt than a slow one. In many claims the pay-dirt is full of large stones and boulders, weighing from one hundred to five hundred pounds each, all of which must be carried away through the sluice. Some are sent down whole, and others are broken into pieces with sledge hammers before they are thrown into the box. These require a swift current and a large body of water. The larger the supply of water, the steeper the sluice is made, other things being equal. Of course economy and convenience of working require that the sluice should be near the level of the ground, and as that may be steep or level below the claim, the grade of the sluice must to some extent conform to it. There are thus a multitude of points to be taken into consideration in fixing the grade of a sluice; but a fall of less than eight or more than twenty inches, in a box of twelve feet, would be considered as unsuitable for the board-sluice. Sometimes the upper part of the sluice is made steeper so as to dissolve the dirt, and the lower part has a small grade to catch the gold. The clayey matter of ordinary pay-dirt is fully dissolved in a sluice two hundred feet long with a low grade, so the use of the boxes beyond that length is merely to catch the gold. There are claims however in which the clay is so extremely tough that it will roll in large balls more than a quarter of a mile through a steep sluice with a large head of water, and come out at the lower end scarcely diminished in size.

The gold is caught in the sluice-boxes by false bottoms of various kinds. It would not do to leave the smooth boards, for the water would sweep all the gold away, and the boards themselves would soon be worn through. The most common false bottom is the longitudinal riffle-bar, which is from two to four inches thick, from three to seven inches wide, and six feet long. Two sets of these riffle-bars go into each sluice-box, the box being twice as long as the bar. A set of riffle-bars is as many as fill one half of a box. They are wedged in, from an inch to two inches apart; the wedging being used, because the bars can more readily be fastened in their places, and more easily taken up, than if nails were used. Before the work of sluicing commences, all the boxes are fitted with riffle-bars, and the bottom of the sluice is therefore full of holes from one to two inches wide, from three to seven inches deep, and six feet long. These are the places in which the gold, quicksilver, and amalgam are caught. Quicksilver is used now in nearly all the sluices, and is the more necessary the smaller the particles of gold. The large pieces of the metal would all be caught by their specific gravity without the aid of amalgamation.

The sluice-boxes having been made, and set up with the proper grade, the water is turned in. The boxes are made of the rough boards as they come from the saw, and the joints are not waterproof, but the leaks are soon stopped by the swelling of the wood, or by the dirt. The stream of water in the sluice is at least two inches deep over the bottom. The height of the sides of the boxes is from eight inches to two feet. The sluice usually runs through the claim, and the auriferous dirt is thrown in with shovels, of which from four to twenty are constantly at work. A man will throw in from two to five cubic yards of dirt in one day. The water rushing over the dirt as it lies in the box, rapidly dissolves the clay and loam, and then sweeps the sand, gravel and stones down. The first dirt in the box goes to fill the spaces between the riffle-bars. After the sluicing has been in progress a couple of hours, some quicksilver is put in at the head of the sluice, and it gradually finds its way downward, most of it stopping, however, near where it is put in.

Amalgamation.—There are a few metals, including gold, silver, copper and tin, which, with quicksilver, form a peculiar chemical union called amalgamation, a process of great importance to the gold miner. When a piece of gold or silver is placed in mercury, the latter metal gradually penetrates through it, destroys the coherence of its particles, and form with it a mass like dough. A lump of gold as large as a bean will be soaked through in three or four days; with silver and copper the process is slower, but they are affected in the same manner. Amalgamation, though a union of a solid with a liquid, differs much from a solution. In the latter the union is mechanical; in the former it is chemical. In the latter the solid is reduced to particles of impalpable fineness; in the former it is not. An ounce of salt will be dissolved in, and nearly equally diffused through, a pint of water; but if an ounce of gold be thrown into a pint of quicksilver, it will, after forming an amalgam with the quicksilver, remain at the bottom. We have no texture so fine that it will strain salt out of water; but the particles of gold are so coarse in amalgam that they can easily be strained out by means of buckskin or tight cloths. However, a little gold will remain in the quicksilver—about the fiftieth part of an ounce of gold in every pound of quicksilver; and the only method of obtaining this gold is by retorting.

Quicksilver is used in gold mining for catching the small particles of metal; the large ones are caught by their weight. But many of the particles are so small that they are almost invisible to the naked eye, and when in moving water they float. Miners frequently show visitors the fineness of their gold by putting some of the dust in a vial with water, and upon shaking, the particles of metal can be seen floating about in the clear water. Riffles, and all the devices to get the benefit of specific gravity, are of little use to arrest this "float-gold," so amalgamation is employed. If a bit of quicksilver is put in the way of the fine gold, the two metals unite at once and make a larger bulk, which can be caught.

There is no such attraction between gold and quicksilver as there is between the magnet and iron; but when the two former metals once touch, an amalgam is immediately formed, and if the proportions of the metals be about even, they in time make a hard mass. Some gold does not amalgamate readily; in various diggings of Siskiyou county, the gold has a reddish coating, which prevents amalgamation. Grease or resin in the water used for washing, is also unfavorable. So is cold. Heat is favorable, and therefore less gold is lost in summer than in winter. Quicksilver that has been once used is considered better than that fresh from the flask.

No tinned iron or copper vessel should be used for holding or panning out amalgam, or dirt containing amalgam; since quicksilver forms an amalgam with tin and copper, and will stick to the sides of a tinned or copper pan.

In most sluices, the quicksilver is put in above the riffle-bars at various places along in the boxes, with a confidence that the great specific gravity of the metal will prevent it from being lost. The greater the quantity and proportion of fine gold, the greater the importance of the quicksilver.

The best method of catching very fine gold by amalgamation is to cover a large copper plate with mercury, and let the dirt and water, in a thickness of not more than a quarter of an inch, pass over it slowly. There are various methods of covering copper plates with quicksilver. The first thing, in every case, is to wash the copper with diluted nitric acid, so as to remove all dirt and grease. The quicksilver may then be rubbed on with a rag; or, still better, it may be dissolved in nitric acid, and the liquid nitrate of quicksilver may be applied with a rag. The nitric acid will attack the copper, and leave the quicksilver as an amalgam on the surface of the copper. This is the most common process, but the nitrate of copper continues for a long time to come up through the quicksilver and interfere with the catching of the gold. When the nitrate of copper appears—it is a green slime—it should be scraped off and the place rubbed over with quicksilver. When a plate is once covered with mercury, the operation need never be repeated; but more mercury must be sprinkled on as the gold collects and forms a solid amalgam. The plate is usually three feet wide and six feet long, and is set nearly level. In very large sluices the stream should be divided so as to run over different plates. The slowness of the current and the shallowness of the water are important, for with a swift current or deep water many of the particles of float-gold may escape without touching the quicksilver. Wherever a speck of gold has fixed itself on the plate, there others will collect about, evidently preferring to fix themselves in a neighborhood rather than in a waste place. The more gold there is on a plate, the better it is considered to be. The seasons for cleaning up are usually determined by the danger of theft. Miners do not like to leave their gold out in quantities so large as to attract thieves. The amalgam is sometimes half an inch thick, and is usually, at cleaning-up time, a hard mass, which must be loosened by heat. The plate is put on a fire, and when it gets so warm that the hand can scarcely bear it, the amalgam is softened and loosened, so that it can be scraped off readily. The plate is then sprinkled anew with quicksilver, and is ready for use again. Mercury does not amalgamate with copper so readily as with gold or silver. A copper plate, the sixteenth of an inch thick, may be used for at least five years, and perhaps for ten; whereas a gold plate of equal thickness would, if exposed to the action of quicksilver in the same manner, fall to pieces in a few weeks. After a time the quicksilver pervades the copper, and gives it a silvery whiteness all through on the under side. It is said that a solution of cyanuret or prussiate of potash, is used instead of nitric acid in applying mercury to copper plates, and that it is still better, there being then no trouble with the green spots of nitrate of copper.

A good amalgamated copper plate is considered as serviceable as a bed of quicksilver of equal size, and it is very much cheaper and more convenient to manage.

The dirt and water should be admitted to the copper plate, by falling first through a sheet-iron plate, pierced with holes half an inch long and a sixteenth of an inch wide. Some miners place this sheet-iron plate immediately over the copper.

Very soon after the water and dirt commence to run in the sluice, all the spaces between the riffle-bars are filled with sand, gravel and dirt; which, however, present many little inequalities of surface, sufficient to catch all the particles of gold larger than a pin-head. The largest gold is caught near the head of the sluice; and the farther down the sluice, the finer the gold. In some sluices, where the pay-dirt contains much coarse gold, the quicksilver is introduced from thirty to sixty yards below the head, so as to catch only the fine particles of metal.

Cleaning up.—The separation of the gold, amalgam, and quicksilver, from the dirt in the bottom of the sluice, is called "cleaning up;" and the period between one "cleaning up" and another is called a "run." A run in a common board-sluice usually lasts from six to ten days. Ordinarily the sluice runs only during daylight, but in some claims the work continues night and day. Cleaning up occupies from half a day to a day, and therefore must not be repeated too often, because it consumes too much time. In some sluices the cleaning up does not occur until the riffle-bars have been worn out or much bruised by the wear of the stones and gravel. Cleaning up is considered light and pleasant work as compared with other sluicing, and is often reserved for Sunday. At the time fixed, the throwing in of dirt ceases, and the water runs until it becomes clear. Five or six sets of riffle-bars, a distance of thirty or thirty-five feet, are taken up at the head of the sluice, and the dirt between the bars is washed down, while the gold and amalgam lodge above the first remaining set of riffle-bars, whence it is taken out with a scoop or large spoon, and put into a pan. Five or six more sets of bars are taken up, and so on down. Sometimes all the riffle-bars are taken up at once, save one set in every thirty-six feet, and then the work of cleaning up is dispatched much more rapidly.

The quicksilver and amalgam taken from the sluice are put into a buckskin or cloth, and pressed, so that the liquid metal passes through, and the amalgam is retained. The amalgam is then heated, to drive off the mercury. This may be done either in an open pan or in a close retort. In the former, the quicksilver is lost; in the latter, it is saved. The pan is generally preferred. Often a shovel or plate of iron is used. Three pounds of amalgam, from which the liquid metal has been carefully pressed out, will yield one pound of gold. The gold remaining after the quicksilver has been driven off by heat from the amalgam, is a porous mass, somewhat resembling sponge-cake in appearance.

Riffle-Bars.—The riffle-bars are usually sawn longitudinally with the grain of the wood, but "block riffle-bars" are considered preferable; the latter are cut across the tree, and the grain stands upright in the sluice-box. The block riffle-bars are three times more durable than the longitudinal; and as the latter kind are worn out in a week in some large sluices, there is a considerable saving in using the former. The block riffle-bars are only two or three feet long.

In some small sluices the riffle-bars are not placed in the boxes longitudinally, nor in sets; but one bar near the head runs downward at an angle of forty-five degrees to the course of the box, not touching its lower end to the side of the box, but leaving an open space of an inch there. Just below this open space another bar starts from the side of the box and runs downward at right angles to the course of the first bar, and an open space is again left at the end of this bar; and so on down to near the lower end of the sluice, where there are longitudinal riffle-bars in sets as described in the preceding paragraphs. The consequence of using this kind of riffle-bar is, that though much of the water and light dirt runs straight over the bars, the heavier material runs down from side to side in a zigzag course. Near the head of the sluice is a vessel, from which quicksilver falls by drops into the box; and it follows the course of riffle-bars, overtaking the gold which takes the same route. These zigzag riffle-bars are nailed down. In all sluices, men must keep watch to see that the boxes do not choke; that is, that the dirt and stones do not collect in one place, so as to make a dam, and cause the water to run over the sides, and thus waste the gold.

There are small sluices, from which all stones as large as a doubled fist are thrown out. For this purpose the miner uses a sluice-fork, which is like a large manure-fork or garden-fork, but has tines which are blunt and of equal width all the way down; the bluntness being intended to prevent the tines from catching in the wood, and the equality of width to prevent the stones from getting fast in the fork.

In some sluices, the "block riffle-bars"—that is, bars cut across the grain of the tree—are set transversely in the boxes, and about two inches apart.

Another device is, to fill the pores of such riffle-bars with quicksilver. This is done by driving an iron cylinder with a sharp edge into the surface of the bar, then putting mercury into the cylinder, and pressing it into the wood. The quicksilver, thus fastened in the wood, catches particles of gold, which must be scraped off when the time for "cleaning up" comes.

Double Sluices.—Sluices are sometimes made double—that is, with a longitudinal division through the middle, so that there are two distinct sluice-boxes side by side. Two companies may be working side by side, so that it will be cheaper for them to build their sluices jointly. In some places the amount of water varies greatly; so that in the winter there is enough to run two sluices, and in the summer only one. And there are companies which wish to continue washing without interruption; so they wash first on one side and then on the other, and clean up without any interruption to the process of washing.

Another device for saving gold in sluices is the "under-current box." There is a grating of iron bars in the bottom of a box, near the lower end of a sluice; and under this grating is another sluice, with an additional supply of clean water, and with a lower grade. The grating allows only the fine material to fall through; and the current of water being moderate, many particles of gold, that would otherwise be lost, are saved. Sometimes the matter from the under-current box is led back to the main sluice.

Rock-Sluices.—Large sluices are frequently paved with stone, which makes a more durable false bottom than wood, and catches fine gold better than riffle-bars. The stone bottoms have another advantage—that it is not so easy for thieves to come and clean up at night, as is often done in riffle-bar sluices. But, on the other hand, cleaning up is more difficult and tedious in a rock-sluice, and so is the putting down of the false bottom after cleaning up. The stones used are cobbles, six or eight inches through at the greatest diameter, and usually flattish. A good workman will pave eight hundred square feet of sluice-box with them in a day; and after the water and dirt have run over them for an hour, they are fastened very tightly by the sand collected between them. In large sluices, wooden riffle-bars are worn away very rapidly—the expense amounting sometimes, in very large and long sluices, to twenty or thirty dollars a day; and in this point there is an important saving by using the stone bottoms. They are used only in large sluices, and they generally have a grade of twelve or fourteen inches to the box of twelve feet.

Hydraulic Mining.—After the board-sluice, with its various adjuncts of riffle-bars, stone bottoms, copper plates, and so forth, the next instrument of importance in the gold-mining of California, is the hydraulic hose, used to let water down from a considerable height, and throw it under the pressure of its own weight against the pay-dirt, which is thus torn down, broken up, dissolved and carried into the sluice below. The sluice is a necessary part of hydraulic mining. The hose is used, not to wash the dirt, but to save digging with shovels, and to carry it to the sluice.

The hydraulic process is applied only in claims where the dirt is deep and where the water is abundant. If the dirt were shallow in the claim and its vicinity, the necessary head of water could not be obtained. Hydraulic claims are usually in hills. The water is led along on the hill at a height varying from fifty to two hundred feet above the bed-rock, to the claim at the end or side of the hill, where the water, playing against the dirt, soon cuts a large hole, with perpendicular or at least steep banks. At the top of the bank is a little reservoir, containing perhaps not more than a hundred gallons, into which the water runs constantly, and from which the hose extends down to the bottom of the claim. The hose is of heavy duck, sometimes double, sewn by machine. This hose when full is from four to ten inches in diameter, and will bear a perpendicular column of water fifty feet high; but a greater height will burst it. Now, as the force of the stream increases with the height of the water, it is a matter of great importance to have the hose as strong as possible; and for this purpose, in some claims, it is surrounded by iron bands, which are about two inches wide, and are connected by four ropes which run perpendicularly down. The rings are about three inches apart. The "crinoline hose," thus made, is very flexible, and will support a column of water one hundred and fifty or two hundred feet high. The pipe at the end of the hose is like the pipe of a fire-engine hose, though usually larger. Sometimes the pipe will be eight inches in diameter where it connects with the hose, and not more than two inches at the mouth; and the force with which the stream rushes from it is so great, that it will kill a man instantaneously, and tear down a hill more rapidly than could a hundred men with shovels.

One or two men are required to hold the pipe. They usually turn the stream upon the bank near its bottom until a large mass of dirt tumbles down, and then they wash this all away into the sluice; when they commence at the bottom of the bank again, and so on. If the bank is one hundred and fifty feet high, the mass of earth that tumbles down is of course immense, and the pipemen must stand far off, for fear that they will be caught in the avalanche. Such accidents are of daily occurrence, and the deaths from this cause probably are not less than threescore every year in the state. Often legs are broken; still more frequently the pipemen have warning, and escape in time. When men are buried in the falling dirt, the water is used to wash them out. In some claims, the pipe will tear down more dirt than the sluice can wash; in other claims, the sluice always demands more dirt than the pipe can bring down. In the latter case, blasting may be used to loosen the dirt, or the miners may undermine the bank, leaving a few columns of dirt for support; and then these being washed away by the pipe, the whole bank comes tumbling down.

In hydraulic claims, all the dirt is washed; in all other kinds of claims, such dirt as contains no gold is thrown to one side, or "stripped off." "Hydraulic mining" is the highest branch of placer mining; it washes more dirt, and requires more water, and a larger sluice, than any other kind of mining. The number of men employed in a hydraulic claim, however, is usually small, from three to six, the water doing nearly all the work. In some claims a man is constantly employed with a heavy sledge-hammer in breaking up large stones, so that the pieces may be sent down the sluice. One man attends to the sluice, and sees that the dirt does not choke up in the sluice, or in the claim above it.

The quantity of dirt that can be washed with a hydraulic pipe depends upon various circumstances—such as the supply of water, the height of its fall, the toughness of the dirt, and the amount of moisture in it. More can be washed in winter than in summer, because the dirt is then moister, and requires less water to loosen and dissolve it. The quantity of water used in a hydraulic claim is from forty to two hundred inches. With one hundred inches, at least thirty cubic yards can be washed in ten hours, on an average; and three men can do all the work. If there were a cent's worth of gold in each cubic foot, the thirty cubic yards would yield eight dollars and ten cents per day, or two dollars and seventy cents to the man, exclusive of the cost of water. But, as a matter of fact, nearly all the hydraulic claims pay more than that, and they will average at least three cents to the cubic foot, and many of them yield five cents. The water usually costs twenty cents an inch per day, so that one hundred inches would cost twenty dollars. Allowing for the water at that rate, a claim in which thirty cubic yards could be washed in a day with one hundred inches of water, and in which the dirt contained five cents to the cubic foot, would leave a net pay of six dollars and sixty-six cents to each man per day.

One hydraulic company, of whose labors I have a note, washed two hundred and twenty-four thousand cubic feet of dirt in six days, using two hundred inches of water, and employing ten men. The wages of the men amounted, at four dollars per day each, to two hundred and forty dollars; the water cost three hundred dollars; and the waste of quicksilver, and wear of sluice, perhaps one hundred dollars more, making a total expenditure of six hundred and forty dollars: and the gold obtained was three thousand dollars, leaving a clear profit of twenty-three hundred and fifty dollars. The dirt contained one cent and a fifth of gold in a cubic foot. The greater the amount of water used, the greater the proportionate amount of dirt that can be washed, and the greater the proportionate profits. It is far more profitable to have a large sluice than a little one, if the water and dirt can be obtained in abundance.

Usually, in a hydraulic claim, the dirt is washed down to the bed-rock; but in some places the washing stops far above the bed-rock, because there is no outlet for the water.

Blasting.—In some hydraulic claims, the dirt, in dry seasons, is blasted, so as to loosen it. A drift or hole is cut into the bottom of a hill, one or two hundred feet high, and a number of kegs of powder (from twenty to two hundred) are introduced, and they are fired with a slow match. The explosion makes an earthquake in the vicinity; and the ground is loosened to such an extent that there is a great saving of labor. The breaking up of the dirt and the exposure to the air are supposed to facilitate the washing greatly.

More water is required for piping down banks than for washing the dirt; and often the sluice is almost idle for want of dirt, while the water, after being thrown against the hillside, runs away without doing any service at washing. Blasting, therefore, by loosening the earth, enables the hydraulic miner to have an abundant and regular supply of dirt in his sluice, at an expense much less than the cost of manual labor to dig the bank down with pick and shovel.

Tail-Sluice.—The tail-sluice is a large sluice made for rewashing the tailings or dirt which has previously passed through other sluices. It is placed ordinarily in the bed of a ravine or creek through which tailings run, and it receives no attention for weeks or months at a time, save to keep it from choking. The sluices emptying into it furnish both dirt and water, and in the dirt there is always a large amount of fine gold, as is plainly proved by the fact that some of the tail-sluices have paid large profits to their owners. Tail-sluices are always large, long and paved with stones; and sometimes they are double, so that one side may be cleaned up while the other continues washing. In a branch of the Yuba there is, or was not long since, a tail-sluice twenty feet wide.

Tunnel-Sluice.—A tunnel-sluice is a sluice in a tunnel. It sometimes happens that a considerable body of water runs out through a tunnel; and in such case, a sluice at the bottom of the tunnel offers the easiest method of getting out and washing the dirt. The tunnels are never cut level, but with a slightly ascending grade, so that the water will always run out. The grade is so low, that transverse riffle-bars must be used; for with longitudinal riffle-bars or stones, there would be too much danger of choking. These tunnel-sluices, because of their low grades, require much more attention than any other kind of sluices.

Ground Sluice.—All the sluices hitherto mentioned and described have wooden boxes, but the ground-sluice has no box: the water runs on the ground. The place selected for the ground-sluice is some spot where there is a considerable supply of water, a steep descent for it, and much poor dirt. The stream is turned through a little ditch, which the miners labor to deepen and enlarge, and when it is deep they prize off the high banks so that the dirt may fall down into the ditch. This is a very cheap and expeditious way of washing, but it is not applied extensively. It is used to the most advantage for washing where the water is abundant for only a few weeks after heavy rains, and where it would not pay to erect large sluices. A few cobble-stones should be left or thrown at intervals in the bed of the ground-sluice to arrest the gold, for if the bed were smooth clay, the precious metal might all be carried off. Quicksilver is not used in the ground-sluice. After the dirt has all been put through the ground-sluice, it is cleaned up in a short board-sluice, or a tom.

Long Tom.—The tom or long tom, an instrument extensively used in the Californian mines in 1851 and 1852, but now rarely seen, is a wooden trough about twelve feet long, eighteen inches wide at the upper end, and widening at the lower to thirty inches, with sides eight inches high. It is used like a board-sluice, but has no riffle-bars, and at the lower end its bottom is of sheet-iron, perforated with holes half an inch in diameter. This sheet-iron is turned up at the lower end, so that the water never runs over there, but always drops down through the perforated sheet-iron or riddle, into a little riffle-box, containing transverse riffle-bars. A stream of water of about ten inches makes a "tom-head"—or the amount considered necessary for a tom—through the tom, which has a grade similar to that of a board-sluice. The dirt is thrown in at the head of the tom, and a man is constantly employed in moving the dirt with a shovel, throwing back such pieces of clay as are not dissolved, to the head of the tom, and throwing out stones. From two to four men can work with a tom; but the amount of dirt that can be washed is not half that of a sluice. The tom may be used to advantage in diggings where the amount of pay-dirt is small and the gold coarse. The riffle-box contains quicksilver, and as the dirt in it is kept loose by the water falling down on it from the riddle above, a large part of the gold is caught; but where the particles are fine, much must be lost.

Cradle.—The rocker or cradle is still less than the tom and inferior in capacity. It bears some resemblance in shape and size to a child's cradle, and rests upon similar rockers. The cradle-box is about forty inches long, twenty wide, and four high, and it stands with the upper end about two feet higher than the lower end, which is open so that the tailings can run out. On the upper end of the cradle-box stands a hopper or riddle-box twenty inches square, with sides four inches high. The bottom of this riddle box is of sheet-iron, perforated with holes half an inch in diameter. The riddle-box is not nailed to the cradle-box, but can be lifted off without difficulty. Under the riddle is an "apron" of wood or cloth, fastened to the sides of the cradle-box and sloping down to the upper end of it. Across the bottom of the cradle-box are two riffle-bars about an inch square, one in the middle, the other at the end of the box. The dirt is shovelled into the hopper, the "cradler" sits down beside his machine, and while with one hand with a ladle he pours water from a pool at his side upon the dirt, with the other he rocks the cradle. With the water and the motion the dirt is dissolved, and carried down through the riddle, falling upon the apron which carries it to the head of the cradle-box, whence it runs downward and out, leaving its gold, black sand, and heavier particles of sand and gravel behind the riffle-bars. The man who rocks a cradle learns to appreciate the fact, that the "golden sands" of California are not pure sand, but are often extremely tough clay, a hopperful of which must be shaken about for ten minutes before it will dissolve under a constant pouring of water. Many large stones are found in the pay-dirt. Such as give an unpleasant shock to the cradle, as they roll from side to side of the riddle-box, are pitched out by hand, and after a glance to see that no gold sticks to their sides, are thrown away; but the smaller ones are left until the hopperful has been washed, so that nothing but clean stones remain in the riddle, and then the cradler rises from his seat, lifts up his hopper, and with a jerk throws all the stones out. The water and the rocking are both necessary. Without the water, the dirt could not be washed; and without the rocking, the dirt would dissolve very slowly, and the gold would most of it be lost. The rocking keeps the dirt in the bottom of the cradle more or less loose, so that the particles of gold can sink down in it, whereas if the cradle stood still, the sand there would almost immediately pack down into a hard floor, over which the gold would run almost as readily as over a board. The whole business of washing with a cradle, is a repetition of the process already described—some dirt, about one-third or one-fourth of what the hopper would hold, if full, is put into the hopper, and while the cradle is rocked with one hand, the other pours in the water. The cradle is cleaned up two or four times in a day. The cleaning up is done by lifting the hopper, taking out the apron, scraping up all the dirt in the bottom of the cradle with an iron spoon, putting it into a pan and washing out the dirt, so that only the gold will be left. This last process is called panning out, and will be described in the next section. Most of the gold collects above the upper riffle-bar, including all the larger lumps. If the apron be of rough woollen cloth, some of the fine gold will be caught there. In diggings where the gold is very fine, the hopper is sometimes placed over the lower end of the cradle, and the apron is made twice as long, and with a lower inclination than in the more common form of the rocker. The water for the cradle should be supplied by a little ditch, with a reservoir at the head of the cradle, to contain five or six gallons. The dipper should be of tin, shaped like a basin, hold about a gallon when full, and have a handle an inch and a half in diameter, and eight inches long. The difference of height between the upper and lower ends of the cradle should not be more than two inches: a steeper inclination will make the current running through it too strong, and the gold will be carried off; and, on the other hand, if the cradle be nearer a level it will be hard to rock, and the dirt in the bottom will pack more rapidly. The amount of dirt that can be washed in a day with a cradle, varies from one to three cubic yards. The dirt is usually shovelled into a pan or bucket, from which it is thrown into the hopper. The miners usually measure the amount of dirt washed by the number of "pans." One man working alone with a cradle ought to wash from seventy-five to one hundred and fifty pans in a day, and two men will wash twice as much. A pan may contain one-third or one-half of a cubic foot. Two men can work more conveniently with the rocker than one. There is enough work to give constant employment to a cradler and a shoveller. The latter has a couple of buckets or pans, which he fills alternately, always keeping one full and near the cradler, so that without moving his feet he can pick it up and empty it into the riddle-box. If the rocker have only one man, he must stop rocking after washing every pan and get more dirt. This delay is injurious to the process of washing, because it allows the dirt in the bottom of the cradle to harden and pack, and some gold is always lost as a consequence. If the dirt and water be convenient, not more than two men can work to a profit with a rocker. But sometimes it happens that water cannot be led to the claim, and in such case the dirt must be carried to the water, a greater weight of which is used than of dirt. At least three times as much water as dirt is required for washing. If the distance from the hole to the water be not over ten or twenty feet, the miners will usually carry the dirt in buckets; if farther they will use wheelbarrows; and sometimes for greater distances pack-mules or waggons. The greater the distance, the more the men required for carrying the dirt. Sometimes, too, it happens that the claim is troubled by water, and then one man may be constantly employed in bailing.

It is of great importance in mining with the cradle, to have the cradle placed within four or five feet of the hole from which the pay-dirt is obtained, and to have a good supply of water at the head of the cradle, and then to have a good descent below the cradle, so that the tailings may all be carried away by the water, so as not to accumulate. The rocker washes about one-half the amount of dirt that can be washed by an equal number of men with the tom, one-fourth of what can be washed with the sluice, and one-hundredth of the amount that can be washed with the hydraulic process; but it is peculiarly fitted for some kinds of diggings. Many little gullies, containing coarse gold in their beds, cannot obtain water for washing except during rains, and then only for a few days at a time. In these gullies the cradle can be used to the best advantage, for it can easily be transported, and it is very good for saving coarse gold. While dirt that would pay from ten to twenty-five cents, was abundant at the surface of the earth in the Californian mines, the cradle was extensively used, but now it has been abandoned by the whites, and is left to the Chinamen, who think themselves doing well if they make seventy-five cents or one dollar per day.

The great difficulty in mining with the cradle is, that the sand will "pack," or make a hard mass on a level with the top of the riffle-bars, and the gold then is lost. So long as the cradle is in motion the dirt does not pack, but when the rocking ceases, the mass hardens in a few minutes. If the miner leaves his cradle standing for fifteen minutes, he stirs up the dirt with his spoon before commencing again to wash. One device to prevent packing is to put a little block under each end of the rockers, so that at the end of every motion the cradle receives a shock. Quicksilver is sometimes used in cradles, but not usually.

Pan.—The pan is used in all branches of gold mining, either as an instrument for washing, or as a receptacle for gold, amalgam, or rich dirt. It is made of stiff tin or sheet-iron, with a flat bottom about a foot across, and with sides six inches high, rising at an angle of forty-five degrees. A little variation in the size or shape of the pan will not injure its value for washing. Sheet-iron is preferable to tin, because it is usually stronger and does not amalgamate with mercury. The pan is the simplest of all instruments used for washing auriferous dirt. Some dirt, not enough to fill it full, is put in, and the pan is then put under water. The water ought to be not more than a foot deep, so that the pan may rest on the bottom, while the miner inserts his fingers in and under the dirt and lifts it up a little, so that the whole mass is wet. If the water be deep, the pan may be held in one hand while the other is used to stir up the dirt, but it is more convenient to take both. The dirt having been filled with water, the miner catches the pan at the sides, raises that part toward his body, and lowers the outer edge a little, and commences to shake the pan from side to side, holding it so that all the dirt is under water, and so that a little of the dirt can escape over the outer edge. The earthy part of the dirt is rapidly dissolved by the water, assisted by the shaking of the pan and the rolling of the gravel from side to side, and forms a mud which runs out while clean water runs in. The light sand flows out with the thin mud, while the lumps of tough clay and the large stones remain. The stones collect on the top of the clay, and they are scraped together with the fingers and thrown out. This process continues, the pan being gradually raised in the water, and its outer edge depressed, until all the earthy matter has been dissolved, and that as well as the stones swept away by the water, while the gold remains at the bottom. Panning is not difficult, but it requires practice to learn the degree of shaking, which dissolves the dirt and throws out the stones most rapidly without losing the gold. If the shaking be too mild and slow, the process consumes too much time; whereas if it be too rapid and violent, the gold is carried off with the stones. Sometimes the pan is shaken so that the dirt receives a rotary motion. This is the most rapid method of washing dirt, but also the most dangerous. The pan must always be used in cleaning up the dirt which collects in the cradle, in prospecting, and frequently in washing small quantities of dirt collected in other kinds of placer mining. Amalgam can be separated from dirt by washing, almost as well as gold. In panning out, it frequently happens that considerable amounts of black sand containing fine particles of gold are obtained, and this sand is so heavy that it cannot be separated from the gold by washing, while it is easily separated by that process from gravel, stones and common dirt. The black sand is dried, and a small quantity of it is placed in a "blower," a shallow tin dish open at one end. The miner then holding the pan with the open end from him, blows out the sand, leaving the particles of gold. He must blow gently, just strong enough to blow out the sand, and no stronger. From time to time he must shake the blower so as to change the position of the particles, and bring all the sand in the range of his breath. The gold cannot be cleaned perfectly in this manner, but the sand contains iron, and the little of it remaining is easily removed by a magnet. The blower should be very smooth, and made of either tin, brass or copper.

Dry Washing.—Dry washing is a method of winnowing gold from dirt. In many parts of the mining districts of California, water cannot be obtained during the summer for mining purposes. The miner therefore manages to wash his dirt without water. He takes only rich dirt, and putting it on a raw hide, he pulverizes all the lumps and picks out the large stones. He then with a large flat basin throws the dirt up into the air, catches it as it comes down, throws it up again, and repeats this operation until nothing but the gold remains. Of course a pleasant breeze, that will carry away the dust, is a great assistance to the operation. Sometimes two men have a hide or a blanket, with which they throw up the dirt. The process is very similar to the ancient method of separating grain from chaff. The miner who devotes himself to dry washing must be very particular to take only rich dirt, so he scrapes the bed-rock carefully. He never digs very deep—not more than twenty feet; and when he goes beyond seven or eight feet he "coyotes," or burrows after the pay-dirt. He may coyote into the side of a hill, or sink a shaft and coyote in all directions from it. This style of mining is named from the resemblance of the holes to the burrows of the coyote, or Californian wolf. Coyoting is not confined to the dry washing, but is used also by miners washing with the pan and cradle. One of the Congressmen elected some years ago to represent California at Washington, was a miner at the time of his nomination, and was so fond of coyoting, that he was generally known as "Coyote Joe."

Dry Digging.—Dry digging is that mining where the miner, after using the shovel to strip off the barren dirt, scrapes the pay-dirt over with a knife, picking out the particles of gold as he comes to them, and throwing away the earthy matter. This is a slow process, but in rich placers may be profitable. The miner is, of course, particular to examine all the crevices in the bed-rock; and if the material be slate, he digs up part of it, to see whether the gold has not found its way into cracks scarcely perceptible on the surface. "Dry digging," as a mode of mining, must not be confounded with "dry diggings," a kind of mining ground which has been described near the beginning of this chapter.

Knife-mining differs a little from dry digging. In the latter, a shovel is used to strip off the barren dirt; whereas the knife-mining is practised in those places where the gold is deposited in crevices in rocks along the banks of streams, without any covering of barren dirt, so that the knife alone is used in scraping out the dirt; and afterward the dirt, being placed in a pan, may be washed in water, which is never used in dry digging.

Puddling-Box.—The puddling-box is a rough wooden box, about a foot deep and six feet square, and is used for dissolving very tough clay. The clay is thrown into the box, with water, and a miner stirs the stuff with a hoe until the clay is all thoroughly dissolved, when he takes a plug from an auger-hole about four inches from the bottom, and lets the thin solution of the clay run off, while the heavier material, including the gold, remains at the bottom. He then puts in the plug again, fills up the box with water, throws in more clay, and repeats the process again and again until night, when he cleans up with a cradle or pan. The puddling-box is used only in small mining operations, and never with the sluice, or in hydraulic claims.

Quicksilver-Machine.—The quicksilver-machine, or Burke rocker, is a cradle about seven feet long, two feet wide, and two feet high. In the bottom are a number of compartments, all containing quicksilver. One man rocks the machine without cessation. A constant stream of water pours into the machine at its head. The riddle extends the whole length of the machine; and the stones, after being washed clean, fall off the riddle at the lower end. One man is employed constantly working with a shovel to keep the dirt on the riddle under the stream of water, and in throwing off the big stones. If the pay-dirt is very convenient, two men can shovel enough to keep the machine in operation. The Burke rocker was extensively used in California eight and ten years ago, but now it is a great rarity.

Tunnel-Mining.—A tunnel, in California mining, is an adit or drift entering a hill-side, or running out from a shaft. Mining-tunnels are usually nearly horizontal—those entering hill-sides having a slight ascent, for the double purpose of draining the mine, and to facilitate the removal of the pay-dirt. In a few hills the tunnels run downward at an angle of twenty degrees or more, to avoid veins or ledges of rock, which would have to be blasted through if the tunnel were cut horizontally; but this can only be done with safety in hills which are drained by older horizontal tunnels.

The mining-tunnel does not run through a hill, but only into it. The length of tunnels varies greatly; the longest are about a mile. The usual height is seven feet, the width five feet. Ordinarily the top must be supported by timbers, to prevent it from falling in, and not unfrequently the sides must also be protected by boards. The cost of cutting a tunnel varies from two to forty dollars a longitudinal foot, according to the nature of the ground, the cost of getting timbers, &c. Tunnels are usually made by companies of eight or ten men, of whom one-half may be merchants, lawyers, physicians or office-holders, and the remainder laboring miners. The latter class do the work; the former furnish provisions and tools, and a certain amount of cash weekly until the pay-dirt is reached. Two or three men work at a time cutting a tunnel; one or two to dig the earth, and one or two to haul it out. The dirt of the first fifty yards is hauled out in a wheelbarrow; beyond that distance a little tram-way or railroad is laid down, and the dirt is hauled out in cars, pushed by the miners. It is not customary to use horses. It is common to have two relays of laborers—one set working from noon to midnight, the other from midnight to noon. Work in a tunnel is as pleasant at night as in the daytime. When a company is rich, or has many laborers, it may have three relays, each to work eight hours in the twenty-four.

It is not uncommon for two companies, owning adjacent claims in a hill, to unite and cut a tunnel on joint account along the dividing line. They go in until they reach the pay-dirt, and then a surveyor is employed to run the line between their claims, and the tunnel is continued through the pay-dirt. The dirt from the tunnel is washed for the joint account of the two companies. After the dividing line has been established, each company keeps on its own side, and each has its time to use the tram-way. They may also have a joint-stock sluice at the mouth of the tunnel—one company having the privilege of using the sluice one week, and the other the next. All the dirt brought out in a week can readily be washed in a day. The work of taking out the pay-dirt after the main tunnel has been cut, is called "drifting;" and the holes made by the men engaged in it are termed "drifts." The drifts are usually not so high as the tunnels. The large stones and barren dirt obtained in the drifts are piled up here and there to sustain the earth overhead. Sometimes wooden posts are likewise necessary.

Shafts.—Shafts are used in prospecting, and also in mining, where the claims are deep and cannot be reached by either the hydraulic process or the tunnel. The prospecting shaft is sometimes sunk into hills supposed to be auriferous, where the shaft is far less expensive than the tunnel. After the shaft demonstrates that the dirt is rich, and precisely the altitude at which it lies, a tunnel is cut to strike it. The shaft may be the cheaper for prospecting, but the tunnel is usually the cheaper if any large amount of dirt is to be taken out.

The shaft is dug by one man in the hole, and one or two are employed at a windlass in hauling up the dirt. Mining-shafts in placer diggings are rarely over one hundred feet deep; but one was dug in Trinity county to the depth of six hundred feet, for the purpose of prospecting, but it found neither pay-dirt nor the bed-rock.

River-Mining.—River-mining is mining for gold in the beds of rivers, below low-water mark. The only practicable method of doing this is by damming the stream, and taking the water out of its bed, in a ditch or flume. It has been proposed by persons who never saw the mines, to get the gold by dredging, or with a diving-bell; but such schemes are absurd in the eyes of miners. The rivers in which the gold is found are mountain-torrents, in which a canoe can scarcely float in summer, much less a dredging machine; and any large scoop working under water would miss the crevices and corners in the rocks, where most of the gold is found. As the water is very seldom more than a couple of feet deep, a diving-bell would be of little service. The flume, the ditch, and the wing-dam, are the chief tasks of the river-miner. The ditch is rarely used, because the banks of the mining-streams are usually so steep, high, rocky and crooked, that a flume is cheaper. The wing-dam is not often used, because the river-beds are in most places too narrow. The flume is almost universally employed.

The work of river-mining can be done only during the summer and fall, while the water is low, and while the miner can have confidence that it will not rise. It may be as low in January as in August, but the winter is the season of rains; and when the flood comes, it sweeps dams, flumes and every thing before it. If the dam and flume be commenced too early in the season, they may be carried off before they are finished; and it frequently happens that they are destroyed in the fall just when the miners are commencing to reap the reward of their summer's labor.

River-mining has many disadvantages, as compared with other branches of mining. The miner cannot work at it more than half the year; he cannot prospect the dirt which is hidden under water; he must erect expensive dams and flumes, which can be used for only a few months; and then he is exposed to floods which may come and destroy all his work before he has commenced to wash. These disadvantages, and the exhaustion of most of the river-diggings in the state, have almost put an end to river-mining in California. In a few cases, extensive fluming enterprises have proved profitable; but, as a general rule, river-mining in this state has cost more than it has produced. A river is seldom flumed for less than three hundred yards, and sometimes for a mile; and the lumber and labor required to make so long a flume, and one large enough to hold all the water of a river, are very expensive. The dam will always leak, and water will run into the bed from the adjacent hills and mountains, and this water must be lifted out by pumps driven by wheels placed in the flume. The river-beds are full of large rocks, weighing from one to ten tons, and these must be moved by machinery, to allow the dirt to be taken out.

River-mining is now never undertaken by an individual, but always by large associations, generally called "fluming companies," sometimes composed of miners exclusively, sometimes of miners and all the principal business-men living near the place where the work is to be done. The lawyers, doctors and office-holders, pay their assessments in cash; the merchants furnish provisions, the lumbermen supply lumber, and the miners make the dam, and help the carpenters build the flume.

Beach-Mining.—Beach-mining is the business of washing the sands of the ocean-beach. Between Point Mendocino, in California, and the mouth of the Umpqua River, in Oregon, the beach-sand contains gold, and in some places it is very rich. The beach is narrow, and lies at the foot of a bluff bank of auriferous sand. In times of storm, the waves wash against this bank, undermine it, sweep away the pieces which tumble down, leaving the gold on the beach. The gold is in very fine particles, and it moves with the heavier sand, which alters its position frequently under the influence of the waves and surf. One day, the beach will have six feet depth of sand; the next, there will be nothing save bare rocks. The sand differs greatly in richness at various times: one day, it will be full of golden specks; a few days later, at the same place it will be barren. The sand in the mean time has been moved by the waves, and replaced by other sand.

It is a very difficult matter to know where the sand is rich and where it is not. The companies employed in mining on the beach number about ten men; and there is a foreman who rides out early every morning, following the beach about two miles to the northward and two miles to the southward of the camp, for the purpose of finding where the sand is the best. So changeable is the sand, that a new examination is made every day; and only three or four men are supposed to be good judges of the quality of sand, from its appearance.

When the foreman has selected a place, he orders all the men to it, and they go with twenty pack-mules, which carry the sand in *alforjas*, or raw hide sacks, to the place of washing, which is up on the bluff, probably a mile or more distant from the spot where the sand is obtained. It happens occasionally that the foreman rides long distances on the beach, and sometimes he will order the sand to be obtained ten miles from the washing-place. The sand must, of course, be very rich, to pay for such transportation, but the beach-sand at times in the sunlight is said to be actually dazzling yellow with gold. The purpose of going upon the bluff to wash it, is to get fresh water for washing; for the sea-water is not so good, nor can it be obtained conveniently. The richest dirt is that the farthest down on the beach, so still weather and low tide are the best times for getting it. When a rich place is discovered low down on the beach, great exertions are made to get as much of the sand as possible before the tide rises. When high tide and storm come together, little can be done. The sand, having been separated from all clay and soluble matter by the action of the sea, is very easily washed, and all collected in a month can be washed in two days in a sluice.

Mining-Ditches. — The placer-mines of California would yield very little gold, were it not for the numerous ditches which supply them with water for washing. The auriferous districts are very dry in summer, and in some places there is not a spring nor a brook within many miles. The artificial ditch supplies the want. The ditches are made by large companies, which sell the water by the "inch." An inch of water is as much as will run out of an orifice an inch square, with the water standing six or seven inches deep in the flume over the orifice. The depth of water over the orifice is called the "head." The orifice is usually two inches high, and as long as necessary to give the amount of water desired. Nobody wants less than ten or twelve inches for mining: a "sluice-head" is about eighteen inches; a "hydraulic-head" is from forty to two hundred inches. The water, however, is not measured accurately. Of course the amount which runs through the orifice will depend to a considerable extent upon the "head," which is usually greater in the morning than at night. At sunrise there may be fifteen inches head, and at sunset only three. The water collects during the night, and is exhausted during the day. The price of water is in no place less than ten cents an inch per day; in some places it is forty cents; the average is about twenty cents.

Many of these ditches are extensive enterprises, and have cost hundreds of thousands of dollars. When they cross ravines and valleys, large flumes—wonders of carpentry—must be built. Some of these are two hundred feet high and a mile long, and so large that a horse and waggon can be driven through them. In all, save length and durability, they are as wonderful as the great Roman aqueducts, whose tall ruins still stand in the Campagna, near the Eternal City. In some cases iron tubes have been used, and although they are very expensive, yet they may pay for themselves, by preventing evaporation, leaking and soaking, which take away much of the water from flumes and ditches.

Prospecting.—"Prospecting" is the search for gold. The instruments used by the prospector for placer-mines are usually the pan, pick and shovel. He should be familiar with the general laws of the distribution of gold, and then try the dirt in the most favorable places. If there is any gold in a district, he can scarcely fail to find specks of it by washing dirt from the bed-rock in the ravines, and in bars. The existence of gold in a district having been established, close observation will suggest to the prospector where he may reasonably expect to find the best diggings. It is usually found that placer-gold is collected in those places where, if he had been familiar with the ancient topography of the country, he should have had reason to suppose that it would be.

Quartz Mining.—Quartz mining differs much from placer mining. For the former, more capital, more experience, more complicated machinery and richer material are required than for the latter. The placer miner throws the dirt into the water, which then does the work; whereas the pulverizing of rock is a nice operation, requiring constant attention. Quartz requires a mill and water-power; placer dirt is washed in a simple sluice. Dirt containing ten cents in the cubic yard may pay the hydraulic miner, but the quartz miner must have a hundred times as much in a cubic yard of vein stone, or he cannot work. The placer gold, when freed from the baser material surrounding it, is much of it in coarse particles, which are easily caught by their specific gravity; the quartz gold must be reduced to a fine powder before it be set free from its gangue, and with the fineness of the particles increases the difficulty of catching them.

Auriferous quartz lodes are often found by accident. Not unfrequently it happens that a rich streak of pay-dirt in a placer claim is followed up to the quartz vein from which it came. While miners are out walking or hunting, they occasionally will come upon lodes in which the gold is seen sparkling. Some good leads have been found by men employed in making roads and cutting ditches. The quartz might be covered with soil, but the pick and shovel revealed its position and wealth. In Tuolumne county in 1858, a hunter shot a grizzly bear on the side of a steep *canon*, and the animal tumbling down, was caught by a projecting point of rock. The hunter followed his game, and while skinning the animal, discovered that the point of rock was auriferous quartz. In Mariposa county, in 1855, a robber attacked a miner, and the latter saw the rock behind his assailant sparkle in the sunlight, at a spot where a bullet struck a wall of rock. He killed the robber, and found that the rock was gold-bearing quartz. In Nevada county, several years ago, a couple of unfortunate miners who had prepared to leave California, and were out on a drunken frolic, started a large boulder down a steep hill. On its way down, it struck a brown rock and broke a portion of it off—exposing a vein of white quartz which proved to be auriferous, induced the disappointed miners to remain some months longer in the state, and paid them well for remaining. Science and experience do not appear to give much assistance in prospecting for quartz lodes. Chemists, geologists, mineralogists and old miners, have not done better than ignorant men and new-comers. Most of the best veins have been discovered by poor and ignorant men. Not one has been found by a man of high education as a miner or geologist. No doubt geological knowledge is valuable to a miner, and it should assist him in prospecting; but it has never yet enabled any body to find a valuable claim.

Distribution of Gold in Quartz.—The rich quartz-veins of California extend from Kern River to the Siskiyou, are found on hills, in *canons* and in vales. They are at least two thousand feet above the level of the sea, and not more than ten thousand feet above it. Their course is generally from north-north-west to south-south-east, and they dip steeply to the eastward, sometimes being nearly perpendicular. They differ in thickness from a line to sixty feet. Quartz veins are very numerous in most of the mining districts, so the task is not to find the veins, but rather to find those which are gold-bearing. It is supposed that nearly all large veins come to the surface of the bed-rock or "country;" but many of them are covered with soil and thus are hidden. Hidden veins are called "blind;" those plainly visible on the surface are called "croppings veins," because their position is shown by the out-croppings. Experience has not ascertained whether large or small veins are more likely to contain gold. It is found in both. The porous quartz, or that containing many cavities, is more frequently found auriferous and richly auriferous, than the very compact quartz. The best gold-bearing veins are usually yellowish or brownish in tinge, near the surface at least; but very rich specimens are found in white and bluish-white rock. Most quartz veins in California contain a little gold; the metal seems to have been distributed most lavishly, but unfortunately in nine-tenths of the veins, the proportion of metal is too small to pay. Most of the large veins are supposed to run for miles upon miles, though they can rarely be traced clearly on the surface for more than a furlong. The auriferous veins vary much in richness. No vein is wrought for more than a few hundred feet. Beyond that, it is either too poor to pay, or the vein is hidden. Some persons have supposed that there is one great gold-bearing quartz vein running along the side of the Sierra Nevada, from Mariposa to Plumas county, and that many of the richest claims are really in this one vein; but this a supposition which cannot be proved now. Sometimes a vein seems to spread out and divide into a number of smaller veins, all of which afterward unite again. These points of junction, and the narrower places in the vein, are usually richer than other parts of it. When two veins cross each other, one may be auriferous on one side of the intersection and not on the other; but in this case the other vein will be auriferous on both sides. It is as though they were streams, one rich, the other barren, and that after meeting, the wealth of the one was divided between them. It is a general rule that metalliferous veins running parallel with the strata of the bed-rock or country are not extensive. In fact they are rather deposits than veins, and though often extremely rich are soon exhausted, while the lodes which run across the stratification, run far and deep, and have a regular and straight course and dip. Lodes lying between two different kinds of rock, are usually richer than those which have the same kind of rock on both sides. Thus it is said that the richest veins of auriferous quartz in California, have been discovered at the intersection of trap and serpentine, and the richest places in veins are where they cross from one kind of bed-rock into another. The richest part of a lode of auriferous quartz is almost invariably on the lower side of the vein, near the foot-wall. All these are facts to be remembered by the prospector as a guide, and an assistance to him in his search for a rich gold-bearing vein. If the lode is covered with earthy matter, he may sometimes trace its course by the difference in the color of the dirt and stones over it from that elsewhere. When the prospector finds dirt and stones on a vein, evidently disintegrated portions of it, he should wash some of the dirt in a pan, and if he finds no gold, there is a strong presumption that the vein is barren.

Prospecting Quartz Rock.—After finding a gold-bearing vein, the question arises whether it will pay. Great sums are lost in gold-mining countries by injudicious investments in mills and machinery to work the auriferous rock, and persons going into the business should be particularly careful not to commit this great error. The business of quartz mining has great profits, but also great pecuniary dangers connected with it. It is rarely that all the rock of a vein will pay for working. In some lodes, the vein-stone will average one hundred dollars to the ton, for all the stone found in a certain part of the lode, but beyond that the rock may be poor or worthless. Picked specimens may be worth several thousand dollars to the ton, but perhaps not more than a ton of such specimens has been obtained in the best lode ever opened in the state. The most profitable lodes are those which have a large supply of rock, easily to be obtained, and all of it yielding something above the cost of working. The common method of ascertaining whether rock will pay, is to pulverize a little of it and wash it in a horn spoon. In taking out the quartz rock in large lodes, it is important to take out only that which will pay, and to determine this, the superintendent of the quarry-men must occasionally test the vein-stone. He takes several little pieces of it, average specimens, places them on a hard, smooth, flat stone, about a foot square, on which he crushes them with a stone muller four inches square, and then by rubbing with the muller he reduces them to a fine powder. He has a horn spoon, made of a large ox-horn, with a bowl about three inches wide, and eight inches long, being merely one-half of the horn in its natural shape. With this spoon he washes out the powder in water, and if he does not find a speck of gold or a "color," as it is called, in a pound of the rock, he infers that it will not pay. The three principal quartz mines in the state are those of Fremont in Mariposa county, of the Allison company in Nevada county, and of the Sierra Butte company in Sierra county. The first has produced $75,000 in a month, the second $60,000, and the third $20,000, but the average is probably thirty per cent. less, and the expenses about thirty per cent. of the total product. The average yield of the Fremont rock is fourteen dollars to the ton, of the Sierra Butte rock eighteen dollars, and that of the Allison company, according to report, has for more than a year at a time been one hundred dollars per ton. The cost of working quartz rock, including quarrying, crushing and amalgamating, is in the best mills from five to ten dollars per ton. The width of the vein, the softness of the rock, the amount of work done, and the skill and industry of the workmen, all are items of great importance in estimating the cost of quartz-mining. It is a business which the owner of the mill ought to understand. The cost of quarrying common quartz rock is about two dollars per ton, that is, for mill-owners that understand the business and superintend the labor themselves. When given out by the job, it usually cost more. When quartz is crushed in a custom mill, that is, a mill built to crush for all applicants, the cost is rarely less than five dollars per ton, and in Washoe, the price was at one time thirty dollars per ton; but in the large mills, where many tons are crushed every day, is about two dollars per ton.

The Divining Rod.—In prospecting for auriferous quartz, use is sometimes made of the divining rod, a practice not without credit with some good miners. The rod is a fork of a green hazel-bush, shaped like a V, with the arms about a foot long. The prospector holds the end of an arm in each hand, with the point of the V directed forward horizontally, and as he walks along, the point turns down whenever he comes over a metalliferous vein, metallic body or water. It is supposed that very few persons can use the divining rod effectually; for most men it refuses to turn. It is used in nearly every civilized country, especially by miners, and is generally considered superstitious, because it is employed by ignorant people, and because there has been no generally accepted scientific explanation of the manner in which a stick could be influenced by a metal hidden under ground. A scientific explanation of the principle of the divining rod has been offered to the world, by Baron Reichenbach, (see page sixty of his *Odic-Magnetic Letters*, translated by John S. Hittel).

Quarrying Quartz.—The quarrying of quartz rock differs little from the quarrying of other metalliferous vein-stones. The lode descends steeply, and the excavation must follow its course. Sometimes the quartz is so soft that it may easily be loosened with the pick. The harder rock is blasted. Soft quartz is that which is penetrated by numerous cavities, though the lumps between the cavities may be very hard. Some quartz on exposure to the air crumbles into sand, though hard when first taken from the vein. In narrow lodes, some of the wall-rock must be cut away to get room for the workmen. In wide lodes, that part of the vein-stone which does not pay is left. Sometimes the gold from the lode penetrates a little way into the foot-wall, and in that case the quarrying must extend beyond the vein stone. The quartz loosened in the vein, must either be hoisted perpendicularly in a bucket with a windlass, or be hauled out through a tunnel. The common method is to hoist the rock with a windlass. Most of the veins are in such places that shafts are more easily dug than tunnels. After the excavation has extended twenty or thirty feet below the surface, it is usual to dig a perpendicular shaft, so as to strike the vein sixty or seventy feet below the surface, and from this point the miner or "drifter" works upward, and as he loosens the rock it falls to the bottom of the shaft, where it is put in the bucket to be hoisted to the surface. Our quartz mines are generally in dry hills, so that they are not troubled much by water; but there are a few shafts where steam-pumps are constantly at work to carry off the water.

Occasionally the miners find small quantities of auriferous quartz which are so easily broken up, and the pieces of gold in which are so coarse, that after the rock has been pounded a little in a mortar, the metal can easily be picked out with the fingers.

Arastra.—Quartz is pulverized either in an arastra, or Chilean mill, or by stamps.

The arastra is the simplest instrument for grinding auriferous quartz. It is a circular bed of stone, from eight to twenty feet in diameter, on which the quartz is ground by a large stone dragged round and round by horse or mule-power. There are two kinds of arastras, the rude or improved. The rude arastra is made with a pavement of unhewn flat stones, which are usually laid down in clay. The pavement of the improved arastra is made of hewn stone, cut very accurately and laid down in cement. In the centre of the bed of the arastra is an upright post which turns on a pivot, and running through the post is a horizontal bar, projecting on each side to the outer edge of the pavement. On each arm of this bar is attached by a chain a large flat stone or muller, weighing from three hundred to five hundred pounds. It is so hung that the forward end is about an inch above the bed, and the hind end drags on the bed. A mule hitched to one arm will drag two such mullers. In some arastras there are four mullers and two mules. Outside of the pavement is a wall of stone a foot high to keep the quartz within reach of the mullers. About four hundred pounds of quartz, previously broken into pieces about the size of a pigeon's egg, are called a "charge" for an arastra ten feet in diameter, and are put in at a time. The mule is started, and in four or five hours the quartz is pulverized. Water is now poured in until the powder is thoroughly mixed with it, and the mass has the consistence of thick cream. Care is taken that the mixture be not too thin, for the thickness of it is important to the amalgamation. The paste being all right, some quicksilver (an ounce and a quarter of it for every ounce of gold in the quartz, and the amount of gold is guessed at from the appearance of the rock) is scattered over the arastra. The grinding continues for about two hours more, during which time it is supposed the quicksilver is divided up into very fine globules and mixed all through the paste (which is so stiff that the metal does not sink in it to the bottom), and that all the particles of gold are caught and amalgamated. The amalgamation having been completed, some water is let in three or four inches deep over the paste, and the mule is made to move slowly. The paste is thus dissolved in the water, and the gold, quicksilver and amalgam have an opportunity to fall to the bottom. At the end of half an hour, or sooner, the thin mud of the arastra is allowed to run off, leaving the precious material at the bottom. Another charge of broken quartz is now put in and the process is repeated, and so on. The length of a "run," or the period from one cleaning up to another, varies much in different places. In the rude arastra a run is seldom less than a week, and sometimes three or four. The amalgam having settled down between the paving stones, the bed must be dug up and all the dirt between them carefully washed. In the improved arastra the paving fits so closely together, that the quicksilver and amalgam do not get down between them, but remain on the surface, and can readily be brushed up into a little pan, and therefore cleaning up is much less troublesome and is more frequently repeated than in the rude arastras; besides there is a greater need of frequent cleaning up in the improved arastras, because the amount of work done within a given time is usually greater.

The arastra is a slow instrument, but in some important respects it is superior to any other method of working auriferous quartz. It grinds the quartz well, is unsurpassable as an amalgamator, is very cheap and simple, requires no chemical knowledge or peculiar mechanical skill in the work, requires but little power, and very little water—all of them important considerations. In many places, the scarcity of water alone is enough to enable the arastra to pay a larger profit than any other method. Again, if a miner finds a rich spot in a lode, he may be doubtful as to the amount of paying rock which he can obtain. Such cases very frequently happen in California, and the arastra is just the thing for the case; for then if the amount of paying rock is small, nothing is lost, whereas the erection of a stamping-mill would cost much time and money, and before it could get into smooth operation the rich rock would be exhausted, and the mill perhaps become worthless. No other simple process of amalgamation is equal to that of the arastra; and it has on various occasions happened in California, that Mexicans making from fifty to sixty dollars per ton from quartz, have sold out to Americans who have erected large mills at great expense, with patent amalgamators, and have not been able to get more than ten or fifteen dollars from a ton. The arastra is sometimes used for amalgamating tailings which have passed through stamping-mills.

Chilean Mill.—The Chilean mill has a circular bed like the arastra, but much smaller, and the quartz is crushed by two large stone wheels which roll round on their edges. In the centre of the bed is an upright post, the top of which serves as a pivot for the axle on which both of the stones revolve. A mule is usually hitched to the end of one of the axles. The methods of managing the rock and amalgamating with the Chilean mill, are very similar to those of the arastra. The Chilean mill, however, is rarely used in California; the arastra being considered far preferable.

Stamps.—Nine-tenths of the quartz crushed in California is pulverized by stamps, of which there are two kinds, the square and rotary. The square stamp has a perpendicular wooden shaft, six or eight feet long, and six or eight inches square, with an iron shoe, weighing from a hundred to a thousand pounds. The wooden shaft has a mortice in front near the top, and a cam on a revolving horizontal shaft enters this mortice at every revolution. When the cam slips out of the mortice, the stamp falls with all its weight upon the quartz in the "battery" or "stamping-box." The rotary stamp has a shaft of wrought iron about two inches in diameter, and just before falling this shaft receives a whirling motion, which is continued by the shoe as it strikes the quartz. The rotary stamp is considered superior to the square, its advantage being that it crushes more rock with the same power, that it crushes more within the same space, and that it wears away less of the shoe in proportion to the amount of rock crushed. There are usually half a dozen square stamps or more, standing side by side in a square-stamp mill, and these do not all fall at the same moment, but successively, running from the head to the foot of the "battery." The quartz is put in at the head of the battery, and is gradually driven to the foot. The rotary stamps sometimes stand side by side, and sometimes in a circle. The battery of both rotary and square stamps is surrounded by wire gauze, or a perforated iron plate, allowing the finely pulverized quartz to escape, and retaining the coarser particles. Quartz is crushed wet and dry. In wet crushing a little stream of water runs into the battery on one side and escapes on the other, carrying all the fine quartz with it.

Separation.—After pulverization comes the separation of the gold from the rocky portion of the powder. The means of separation are mechanical or chemical. The chemical process is amalgamation; the mechanical are those wherein the gold is caught on a rough surface with the aid of its specific gravity. The chief reliance is upon amalgamation, and in some large quartz-mills mechanical appliances are not used at all for catching the particles of gold, but only for catching amalgam.

The mechanical appliances used in quartz-mills in separating the gold from the pulverized rock, are the blanket, the sluice, and the raw hide.

The blanket is a coarse, rough, gray blanket, which is laid down in a trough sixteen inches wide and six feet long. The pulverized quartz is carried over this by a stream of water, and the particles of gold are caught in the wool. The blanket is taken up and washed, at intervals depending upon the amount of gold deposited. In some mills where a large amount of rock is crushed, and where the powder is taken over the blanket before trying any other process of separation, the washing takes place every half hour. In mills where the pulverized quartz is exposed to amalgamation first, the blanket may be washed three or four times a day. The washing is done in a vat, kept for that especial purpose.

The sluice used in quartz-mills is similar to the placer board-sluice, but the amount of matter to be washed is less, and there is no dirt to be dissolved, and there are no larger stones, and therefore the sluice is not so large, so strong, or so steep in grade, as the placer-sluice, and the riffle-bars are not so deep. In some quartz-mill sluices there are transverse riffle-bars. If the quartz has much iron or copper pyrites, the sluice is used to collect this material and save it for separation at some future time. The pyrites ordinarily contains, or is accompanied by much gold, which it protects from amalgamation. This separation of the pyrites from the pulverized rock is called "concentrating the tailings," and the material collected is called "concentrated tailings." In the sluices of some quartz-mills cast iron riffle-bars are used; cast in sections about fifteen inches square, and about an inch deep. Much study has been devoted to the subject of making these riffle-bars in such a manner that the dirt will not pack in them, but will always remain loose, and keep in constant motion under the influence of the water running over them; but the object has never been fully attained. Quicksilver is used in nearly all quartz-mill sluices.

The raw hide used in separating gold from the pulverized quartz is a common cow hide, laid down in a trough with the hairy side up, and the grain of the hair against the course of the water. The gold is then caught in the hair. Sheep hides have been used in the same manner, recalling to mind the Golden Fleece. The hides, however, are inferior to the blankets for this purpose, and are never used in the best mills.

The methods of amalgamating are numerous. Among them are amalgamation in the battery, amalgamation with the copper plate, amalgamating bowls, and patent amalgamation of many kinds.

In many mills quicksilver is placed in the battery, two ounces of quicksilver for one of gold; and about two-thirds of the gold is caught thus. The copper plate in quartz-mills is made in the same manner as in placer-sluices, under which head a description of the plate may be found. Some amalgamating bowls or basins are little Chilean mills and arastras, made of cast iron. One plan of amalgamation is to use a cast iron bowl about four feet in diameter and a foot deep. Near the bottom are horizontal iron arms, which revolve and stir the quicksilver and pulverized quartz together. Four or five of these bowls sit in a row but at different levels: the bottom of the first bowl being level with the top of the second, and so on. The pulverized quartz passes through them all. Under each bowl a fire is kept up, because heat forms the action of amalgamation. If there be any pyrites in the quartz, some common salt is thrown in to assist in releasing the gold from the embraces of the sulphurates, and preparing it to be seized by the mercury. Another amalgamating bowl revolves on an axis that stands at an angle of about seventy-five degrees to the horizon, so that the material in the bowl is continually moving; and the bottom is divided by little compartments, which make a constant riffle. In other bowls the pulverized quartz is forced with water through the mercury. The methods of amalgamation differ very much, and a book might be filled with a description and discussion of the processes used at different quartz-mills in California.

Sulphurets.—Many auriferous quartz veins contain considerable quantities of sulphurets or pyrites of iron, copper and lead, and their presence prevents amalgamation, and thus causes a great loss of gold. It is said that on some occasions in good mills, not more than twenty or thirty dollars have been obtained from a ton of vein-stone which had seven or eight hundred dollars of gold in every ton. The best method of treating the quartz containing pyrites, is to roast it, and thus drive off the sulphur, but this process is so expensive that it is seldom used; and the common practice is to crush and amalgamate the rock, and save the concentrated tailings for some future time, when there may be a sale for them, or when it will be cheaper to reduce them. The pulverized sulphurets are decomposed by exposure to the air, and after the tailings have been preserved for a time, they may pay better at the second amalgamation than at the first. A mixture of common salt assists the decomposition of the pyrites.

Chief Quartz-Mills.—The most productive quartz-mill in the state is the Benton mill, on Fremont's Ranch, in Mariposa county. It is also the largest, having forty-eight stamps. There are four mills on the estate, with ninety-one stamps in all, and their average yield per month is sixty thousand dollars. A railroad four miles long, conveys the quartz from the lode to the mills. The Allison quartz mine in Nevada county, produces forty thousand dollars per month. The Sierra Buttes quartz-mill, twelve miles from Downieville, yields about fifteen thousand dollars per month. These last mills run night and day, and crush and amalgamate ten thousand tons of rock a year, or twenty-eight tons per day. Forty men are employed, twenty-five to quarry the rock, five in the mill to attend to the stamps and amalgamation, one to do carpentry, one for blacksmithing, and eight for getting out timber, transporting quartz, and so forth. The cost of quarrying, crushing and amalgamating a ton of rock, is six dollars. The wages of the men are from fifty to seventy dollars per month with boarding. The average wages is sixty dollars. About ten miles eastward of Sonora, in Tuolumne county, are some rich veins of auriferous quartz, the most prominent of which are the Soulsby and Blakeslee lodes. The Soulsby mill produced forty thousand dollars in three weeks, when it commenced work in 1858, but it has not been so profitable of late.

Silver Mining.—Silver mining has not yet been established fairly as a business in California. The silver ores of Washoe were discovered in 1859, and mining has been fairly commenced there, but the mines of Esmeralda and Coso, within the limits of this state, were not found until the summer of 1860, and up to the present time no mills have been established there.

Silver mining differs much from gold mining. Gold is always found as a metal, never as an ore, and the separation from the accompanying vein-stone with which it is mixed mechanically, is much more simple and easy than the reduction of the argentiferous ores in which the silver is chemically combined with base substances, for which it has a strong affinity. Chemical knowledge and chemical processes are more necessary in mining for silver than for gold; and while all auriferous quartz is of the same kind, and may be treated in the same manner, there are many different kinds of silver ores, each of which requires a peculiar treatment. The reduction of silver ore costs on an average, from three to five times as much as the reduction of auriferous quartz.

The silver ore of Esmeralda and Coso is a sulphuret of silver, nearly all the veins having the same material, though the amount of it scattered through the vein-stone differs greatly in different lodes. In some veins there is much free gold, that is, little specks of metallic gold which can be separated from the other material in the same manner that gold is separated from auriferous quartz. The methods of reducing silver ore are so numerous and complex, and vary so much in different districts and under different circumstances, that it is impossible to know now what process will be used in Esmeralda and Coso, the resources of which places have been so little studied. Besides it is said that new processes for reducing silver ore have been invented, far superior to all the old methods; and these processes are kept secret. It is therefore unnecessary that I should go into a long description of the various processes practised elsewhere. Silver ore after pulverization is smelted by mixing with it fifty per cent. of lead in metal or ore, and ten per cent. of iron, and exposing the whole to a heat sufficient to melt the silver which runs off. The metal thus obtained is not pure but contains much lead, which is driven off by heat while the silver is kept in a molten condition for a period of four or six hours. The cost of smelting in California at present, is about one hundred and twenty-five dollars per ton. In most of the other methods of reducing silver ore, the ore is roasted to drive off the sulphur. In the barrel amalgamation, which has been used at Washoe, and will probably be used at Esmeralda also, half a ton of ore, after being pulverized and roasted, three hundred pounds of water, and one hundred pounds of wrought iron, in little fragments, are put into a barrel, which revolves on a perpendicular axis. At the end of two hours the mass has taken the consistence of thick cream, when five hundred pounds of quicksilver are put in, and after the barrel has revolved four hours more, the amalgamation is complete. More water is now poured in; the barrel revolves very slowly to let the amalgam all settle to the bottom, the mud runs off through a cock four inches above the bottom, and the mercury and amalgam are then drawn off through a little hole in the bottom of the barrel.

Quicksilver Mining.—The ore from which quicksilver is obtained is a sulphuret. The sulphur is driven off by heat, and the metal, which rises in fumes from the ore, is collected by condensation. The miners are Cornishmen and Mexicans. The ore is in large masses underground, not in a connected vein of regular thickness; and after one mass is exhausted, much labor is often vainly spent in search of another. There are, however, usually little seams of ore running from one large deposit to another, and it is the business of the mining captains to observe these veins closely, and trace them up when a "fault" occurs. There are no scientific rules for finding the ore; and the business of searching for the large deposits is never intrusted to educated mining engineers, but always to mining captains, who have themselves been laborers, and have learned by experience where to seek. The New Almaden mine produces two hundred and twenty thousand pounds of metal in a month. The *hacienda*, or reducing establishment of the mining company, has fourteen brick furnaces, each fifty feet long, twelve feet high, and twelve feet wide. At one end of each furnace is the fire chamber, which may be nine cubic feet inside; next to that is the ore chamber of about the same size; and beyond that is the condensing chamber, in which there are a number of partitions alternately running up from the bottom and down from the top, with a space for the fumes to pass, their course being up and down, and up and down again, and so on, for a distance of thirty feet to the chimney, which is forty feet high. In the bottom of the condensing chamber is water. The walls between the fire chamber and the ore chamber, and between the latter and the condensing chamber, are built with open spaces, so that the heat, smoke and fumes can pass through. The ore is placed in the ore chamber in such a manner as to leave many open spaces. The heat drives off the sulphur and mercury of the ore in fumes, which in passing through the condensing chambers, deposit the mercury, and the smoke and sulphur escape through the chimney. In the Enriqueta and Guadalupe mines the quicksilver is condensed in a close iron retort, and the sulphur is absorbed by quicklime.

Copper ore is dug from several mines in California, but it is all exported to be smelted elsewhere.

Platinum. —Platinum, iridium and osmium, three white metals of about the same specific gravity with gold, are found with the latter metal in the placers in the basin of the Klamath and Trinity Rivers. Their particles are usually fine scales, very rarely reaching a quarter of an ounce in weight, and the largest piece of either ever found was less than an ounce and a half. They cannot be separated from the gold by washing, but they do not unite with quicksilver, and therefore they are separated from the more precious metal by amalgamation. They have no regular market in the state; miners never make them the chief object of search, and they have not been studied, so it is not known to what extent they might be obtained.

Del Norte and Klamath. —Del Norte county in the north-western corner of the state, is about forty miles long from east to west by thirty from north to south. The mining population in it is small. Most of the mining is done along the banks of the Klamath River, which runs about twenty miles through the south-eastern portion of the county. There are some miners on the head-waters of Althouse Creek, which runs northward into Oregon. The county assessor, in his report for 1860, does not mention the existence of any quartz-mill or mining-ditch in the county. The mining districts are very mountainous and difficult of access. They obtain most of their supplies from Crescent City. The mining is chiefly in shallow placers, in deep and narrow ravines, and on bars of the Klamath River.

Klamath county lies immediately south of Del Norte, and is about the same size. It is almost exclusively a mining county, and has a population of about eighteen hundred. The diggings are placers in the bars and banks of the Klamath River and its tributaries, the Trinity and Salmon Rivers, and many small creeks. The principal mining places are Orleans Bar, Gullion's Bar, Negro Flat, Cecilville, Weitspeck and Red Cap. The whole county is very rugged and mountainous, and much of it is covered with heavy timber. The diggings are so difficult of access, and are so protected by mountains against ditches, that they will last for many years. There is probably no part of the state where the single miner, without capital, has a better chance to dig gold with a profit. Nearly the whole beach of the county is auriferous.

Siskiyou. —Siskiyou county lies east of Del Norte and Klamath, is forty miles wide from north to south, one hundred miles long from east to west, and reaches to the eastern boundary of the state. It has a population of 7,629, the large majority of whom are engaged in mining. The mining district is all in the western end of the county, along the banks of the Klamath River and its tributaries, the Scott and Shasta Rivers. The Klamath runs through a deep *canon*; the Scott and Shasta Rivers, have pleasant open valleys, but the diggings along their banks are chiefly among the *canons* near the Klamath. Hydraulic and tunnel claims are rare. There are six quartz-mills in the county, and fifteen mining ditches, of which last the principal is the Yreka canal, forty miles long, bringing water from the head of Shasta River to the town of Yreka. In 1859, there were four quartz-mills in the county, one of which was at Mugginsville, one in Scott's valley and two in Quartz valley. I have no information about the situation of the two built since that time. The principal mining towns are Yreka, Scott's Bar, Hawkinsville, Johnson's Bar, Deadwood and Cottonwood.

Trinity and Shasta.—South of the western part of Siskiyou and the eastern part of Klamath, lies Trinity county, ninety miles long from north to south, and about twenty miles wide on an average. The northern part of the county is the basin of the Trinity River, and is auriferous. From the county assessor's report for 1860, it is to be inferred that there is not a quartz-mill or a mining-ditch in the state. The county is very mountainous, and most of the mining is done in rugged *canons* along the Trinity River. The chief mining towns are Weaverville, Cox's Bar, Big Bar, Arkansas Flat, Mooney's Flat and Trinity Centre.

South of Siskiyou and east of Trinity lies Shasta county, which is on an average forty miles wide from north to south and one hundred miles long, reaching to the eastern border of the state. There is a rich auriferous district about twenty miles square, in the vicinity of the town of Shasta, in the south-western part of the county. The diggings are mostly in the basins of Clear Creek, Cottonwood Creek, Rock Creek and Salt Creek, all of which enter into the Sacramento. There are four quartz-mills in the county, one at French Gulch, one at Middle Creek, one at Muletown, and one at Old Diggings. The county has twenty-seven mining ditches, with a joint length of one hundred and forty-one miles, an average of five miles each. The chief mining towns are Shasta, Horsetown, French Gulch, Muletown, Briggsville, Whiskey and Middletown.

Plumas and Sierra.—South of the eastern part of Shasta county lies Plumas, which is about seventy miles square. About one third of the county, in the south-western part of it, comprising that portion drained by the head waters of Feather River, is auriferous. It lies high above the level of the sea, and the work of mining is interrupted during a considerable portion of the winter, by cold, snow and ice. Hydraulic and tunnel claims in deep hills, furnish a large portion of the gold yield of the county. There are five quartz-mills, one at Elizabethtown, one at Eureka Lake, and three at Jamison Creek. The principal mining towns are Quincy, Jamison City, Indian Bar, Nelson's Point and Poorman's Creek.

South of Plumas is Sierra county, which is fifty miles long from east to west, and twenty miles wide from north to south. The North Fork of the Yuba River runs through its centre, and the Middle Fork is its southern boundary. Though small, it is one of the richest mining counties of the state, and in proportion to the extent of its mining ground, is much richer than any other county. All its territory is four thousand feet above the sea level, at the lowest. Most of the mining is done in hydraulic and tunnel claims in deep hills. Near the centre of the county is a mountain called the Downieville Butte, or the Yuba Butte, eight thousand eight hundred and forty-six feet high, on the sides of which are found some rich quartz leads. In 1859 there were eleven quartz-mills in Sierra county, of which seven are at the Butte, two at Downieville, one at the Mountain House, and one at Sierra City. The principal mining towns are Downieville, Monte Cristo, Pine Grove, St. Louis, La Porte, Poker Flat, Eureka City, Forest City, Alleghany Town, and Cox's Bar. One of the most remarkable features of the placers of the state, is the blue lead, which was first discovered in Sierra county, and has been more thoroughly examined there than elsewhere. The "blue lead" is a stratum of blue clay very rich in gold. It is found deep under other strata. The general opinion is, that the blue lead occupies the bed of a large antediluvian river, which ran parallel with the Sacramento and about sixty miles eastward of it. It has been traced twenty miles or more, passing near Monte Cristo, Alleghany Town, Forest City, Chip's Flat and Zion Hill. Mr. C. S. Capp wrote thus to the San Francisco *Bulletin*:

"This is not one of the many petty leads, an inch or two in breadth and thickness, which, after being traced a few hundred feet, end as suddenly and mysteriously as they commence; but it is evidently the bed of some ancient river. It is often hundreds of feet in width, and extends for miles and miles, a thousand feet below the summits of high mountains, and entirely through them. Now it crops out where the deep channels of some of the rivers and ravines of the present day have cut it asunder; and then, hidden beneath the rocks and strata above it, it only emerges again miles and miles away. Wherever its continuity has been destroyed, the river or gulch which has washed a portion of it away, was found to be immensely rich for some distance below, and the materials of which the lead is composed are found with the gold in the bed of the stream. It is evidently the bed of some ancient stream, because it is walled in by steep banks of hard bed-rock, precisely like the banks of rivers and ravines in which water now runs, and because it is composed of clay which is evidently a sedimentary deposit, and of pebbles of black and white quartz, which could only be rounded and polished as they are by the long continued action of swiftly running water. The bed-rock in the bottom of this lead is worn into long smooth channels, and also has its roughness and crevices like other river beds. The lighter and poorer qualities of gold are found nearest to its edges, while the heavier and finer portions have found their way to the deeper places near the centre. Trees and pieces of wood, more or less petrified and changed in their nature, which once floated in its waters, are also every where encountered throughout this stratum.

"The clay and fine gravel in which these pebbles and boulders are found to be tightly packed, is of a light-blue color, which gives the name to the lead. Much of this clay is remarkably fine and free from coarse particles, and is smooth and unctuous to the touch. It is said to be strongly impregnated with arsenic, as was shown by chemical analysis, and contains large quantities of iron and sulphur in solution, for pyrites and sulphurets of iron are deposited in shining metallic crystals in every vacant crevice. Fine gold is found among this clay, and the heavier particles beneath it, upon the bed-rock. This stratum varies in thickness from eighteen inches to eight or ten feet, while the whole lead varies in width from a hundred and fifty to five hundred feet.

"The same lead has been found at Sebastopol, four miles above Monte Christo, and also higher up among the mountains. It appears at Monte Christo, which is four miles above the high-lying Downieville, and over three thousand feet above it, and at Chapparal Hill on the side of a deep ravine; then at the City of Six, which is also on very high land, about four miles from Downieville, across the North Yuba. It is next found at Forest City, on both sides of a creek, and is there traced directly through the mountain to Alleghany Town and Smith's Flat, on the opposite side. There it is again cut in twain by a deep ravine. It crops out on the other side at Chip's Flat, where it has been followed by tunnels passing completely through the mountain to Centreville and Minnesota on the other side. Here it is obliterated by the Middle Fork of the Yuba, but it is believed to be again found at Snow Point, on the opposite side of the river, and again at Zion Hill, several miles beyond. There is no reason for doubting that after thus reaching over twenty miles, it still extends further. Hundreds of tunnels have been run in search of it. Where the line it follows was adhered to, they have always found it, and have been well rewarded for their labor. Millions of dollars have been taken from this lead, and its richness, even in portions longest worked, is yet undiminished. These tunnels have cost from $20,000 to $100,000 each, and interest in the claims they enter sell readily at from $1,000 to $20,000, in proportion to the amount of ground within them remaining untouched, and the facilities which exist for working it. Many of these claims will yet afford from five to ten or more years' profitable labor to their owners, before the lead itself within them is exhausted. As in some of them quartz veins and poorer paying gravel have been found, many of them may be valuable to work from the top down as hydraulic claims."

This idea that the blue lead occupies the bed of an antediluvian river is however not universally accepted. Mr. B. P. Avery, who has written numerous newspaper articles upon the mineral deposits, asserts that the "blue lead," as it is called, is not a "lead" but an extensive stratum which is many miles wide, and is found all the way from the foot hills to the summit of the Sierra Nevada. In reply to this, it is said that while a bluish stratum of clay similar to that of the blue lead is found over a wide district, that it is evidently different in origin from the blue lead itself, which is confined to a narrow bed, and marked by the signs found in all the other ancient river beds of the state.

The Sierra Butte Quartz Mining Company has some of the best auriferous quartz lodes in the state. One lode called the Cliff Ledge, is twenty-five feet wide; and another called the Aërial Ledge, is about three feet wide. In the Cliff Ledge, the paying rock averages about six feet in thickness next the foot wall. The average yield is eighteen dollars per ton. The quartz is bluish white in color, and very hard when first taken from the lode, but on exposure to the air it slowly crumbles into sand.

Yuba and Butte.—West of Sierra county, and drained by the same streams, is Yuba, which reaches to the Sacramento River, lying half in the mountains and half in the plains, the mining district being in the former half. The principal mining towns are Camptonville, Timbuctoo, Foster's Bar, Texas Bar and Long's Bar. In 1859 there were nine quartz-mills in the county, three at Brown's valley, and one each at Camptonville, Dobbin's Ranch, Dry Creek, Honcut, Indiana Creek and Robbin's Creek. The assessor in 1860 reported only two quartz-mills in the county. There are twenty-two ditches in the county, with an aggregate length of nine hundred and fifty-two miles, an average of forty-three miles each. The most important ditch, called "Bovyer's," supplies Timbuctoo with five thousand inches of water in the winter, less in the summer. The diggings at Timbuctoo are in a deep hill, which is washed away by the hydraulic process.

West of Yuba and Plumas counties lies Butte, which is drained by the Feather River. The principal mining towns are Oroville, Bidwell's Bar, Forbestown, Natchez and Whiterock. In 1859 there were seventeen quartz-mills in the county, of which four were at Oregon Gulch, at Columbiaville and Hansonville, three each, two at Yankee Hill, and at Evansville, Gold Run, Long Bar, Nesbitt's Flat and Spring Valley, one each. The assessor reports for 1860, twenty-nine quartz-mills, worth fifty thousand dollars, and crushing in the aggregate one hundred and sixty-two and a half tons per day. There are sixty-four mining-ditches, with an aggregate length of five hundred and eighty-three miles. The bars and beds of Feather River were once very rich, and some of the most extensive enterprises of river mining in the state have been undertaken within the limits of Butte county. The greatest flume ever built in California was that of the Cape Claim Company, near Oroville, in 1857. It was three quarters of a mile long and twenty feet wide, and furnished employment for two hundred and fifty men from May till November. The expenditures during that period were $176,985, and the receipts $251,426, showing a clear profit of $74,441. The next year, after the water had fallen, the company commenced its labors again; spent $160,000 and received $115,000, and thus lost $45,000. North of Oroville is a "table-mountain" with a top of basalt, covering a rich deposit of auriferous clay.

Nevada and Placer.—South of Yuba and Butte is Nevada, the richest mining county of the state. Within its limits the tom, sluice, under-current sluice, and crinoline hose were invented, and the ditch and hydraulic power were first applied to placer-mining; and quartz-mining was first undertaken extensively. In 1859 there were thirty-two quartz-mills in the county, and twenty-eight mining-ditches, with an aggregate length of three hundred and ninety-four miles. No part of the mineral region of the state is better supplied with water than Nevada county. The richest quartz district is in the vicinity of Nevada City, which has fifteen mills, and Grass Valley, five miles distant, has seventeen. The great Allison mine, which has the richest lode in the state, is in Grass Valley.

The quartz mines here are much troubled with water, and during the winter of 1860-61, many of the mills were compelled to stop for weeks until the shafts could be drained by steam engines, after having been filled by a long and heavy rain. The annual gold yield of Grass Valley has been estimated at four millions of dollars. North San Juan has the finest hydraulic claims, and Sweetland the largest tail-sluices. The Eureka Lake Ditch Company has more ditching and water than any other company in the state. Their main ditch is seventy-five miles long, and there are one hundred and ninety miles of branches, making a total of two hundred and sixty-five miles, which have cost nine hundred thousand dollars. The daily sale of water is six thousand inches, with a weekly income of six thousand dollars. The principal mining towns are Nevada, Grass Valley, North San Juan, Rough and Ready, Orleans Flat, Moore's Flat and Humbug City.

INDEX